KINGDOMS OF AFRICA

By Stuart Kallen

ABDO
& Daughters

Visit us at
www.abdopub.com

Published by ABDO Publishing Company, 4940 Viking Drive, Edina, MN 55435.
Copyright © 2001 by Abdo Consulting Group, Inc. International copyrights reserved
in all countries. No part of this book may be reproduced in any form without
written permission from the publisher.

Printed in the United States.

Edited by: Paul Joseph
Graphic Design: City Desktop Productions

Cover Photos: Corbis
Interior Photos: Corbis

Library of Congress Cataloging-in-Publication Data

Kallen, Stuart A., 1955-
      Kingdoms of Africa / Stuart Kallen
          p.   cm. - - (Black History)
      Includes index.

      ISBN 1-57765-465-X
      1. Africa--History--To 1884--Juvenile literature. 2.. Ethnology--
Africa--Juvenile literature. [1. Africa--History.]   I. Title.

DT25 .K37 2001
960'.2--dc21   00-056891

CONTENTS

A statue of
the explorer
Vasco da Gama
at the port town
of Sines.

INTRODUCTION

For hundreds of years, Africa and its people have been a mystery to the rest of the world. Early European explorers reported tall, stone cities of wealth and comfort along Africa's East Coast. They went ashore and found people who knew as much about the stars and planets as they did. Vasco da Gama was a Portuguese explorer who traveled to Africa in 1497. He reported that the Africans that he met were very civilized. In fact, they sometimes snubbed the Europeans for behaving rudely.

In 1518, an explorer told Pope Leo X about the ancient African city of Timbuktu. The city had so many scholars, the explorer said, that their major business was selling books.

A stone sculpture of the head of the Portuguese explorer Vasco da Gama.

But Europeans began to think differently about Africa after the slave trade began. This was in the late 1400s. Once Europeans started kidnapping Africans and selling them as slaves, much of Africa was changed forever. The Europeans also distorted facts about Africa and made up lies to justify their actions. Today, scholars and scientists are finally learning the truth about ancient Africa.

The people of Africa have had a long and exciting history. The early Africans created cultures, civilizations, and ideas that were the equal of any in the world. Their passionate spirituality helped them to create artwork and music that were unique and beautiful.

In this book, we will discover the glorious cities and the amazing civilizations that existed in Africa before the Europeans arrived.

Mosque in Kano, Nigeria, the oldest city in West Africa.

CHAPTER 1

THE ROOTS OF HUMANITY

The Bones of Our Ancestors

About 33 million years ago, a nine-pound animal climbed through the trees in a tropical forest in North Africa. This fruit-eating creature had limbs like a monkey and teeth like an ape. Although the animal looked more like a cat, its bone structure was related to the bone structure of humans. The remains of this animal were discovered in 1985. It is the oldest direct ancestor of human beings. Scientists call it the "dawn ape."

About 1.6 million years ago, a 12-year-old boy drowned in the mud and reeds surrounding Lake Turkana, in what is now Kenya. Centuries passed as hippopotamuses and elephants trampled the boy's bones into the mud. In 1984, the bones were found and pieced together by anthropologists. (Anthropologists are scientists who dig up fossils and study ancient human cultures.) The boy's skeleton is the best preserved and most complete skeleton of an early human being ever found.

Because of these and other discoveries, anthropologists believe that every human on Earth has its roots in Africa. The exact birth of

Close-up of ancient hand-held tool.

humankind is still a mystery. But scientists are sure that humanlike creatures were using fire and making tools in Africa millions of years ago.

Early humans continued to change and evolve through ice ages, floods, fires, and great droughts. Around 12,000 years ago, human beings that were much like modern people lived in Africa. These people had stone tools, knew how to trap and kill animals for food, and even had pets. Early humans made paintings on the walls of caves. They also made pottery and built homes that archaeologists (scientists who study ancient people and their cultures) are studying today.

The Climate Changes

Around 8,000 years ago, most Africans lived in the area that is now called the Sahara Desert. But in those days, the climate there was very wet. The land was covered with fertile soil and green plants. Lush, green forests teemed with animals of all sizes. Hundreds of rivers splashed with fish. In this area, which was roughly the size of the United States, modern African culture was born. Hunters, farmers, and herdsmen roamed the land. Many of these people lived in caves, where they painted images on the walls. Hundreds of these beautiful cave paintings still exist today. They show beautiful portraits of men and women, pictures of African gods and goddesses, scenes of warfare, and peaceful villages. Thousands of years old, these paintings provide one of our oldest records of human life.

Approximately five or six thousand years ago, the climate of this part of Africa began to change. The long period of rain and fertility ended. The land began to dry up. Slowly, vast grasslands turned into sandy deserts. By 1500 B.C., the region was covered by desert. The fish and animals died, and the people who hunted them were forced to search for food in other places.

These people moved in three different directions. Each group took along their customs, their memories, and their gods. One group

Detail of a relief of the God Thoth at Karnak, Egypt.

The Sphinx against the pyramid of Cheops in Giza, Egypt.

traveled to the fertile land along the Nile River in southern Egypt. There, they merged with the cultures that built the gigantic pyramids of Egypt. Another group moved farther north and merged with the people around the Mediterranean Sea. Others went south into the heart of the wild African continent.

The Sahara Desert

When the rain stopped falling, around 5,000 years ago, the Sahara Desert began to grow. Blowing sand and rocky ground covered huge

Sahara Desert

11

Mountain rain forest

pouring rain flooded the countryside. The mountains were covered
with thorns and rocks that baked in the awesome heat.

Many Americans think that all of Africa's land is covered by lush
jungle. Actually, these tropical forests take up only a small part of
the African continent. But these places captured the imaginations of
explorers. The tropical forests of Africa were dark, wet places full of
danger and disease. Rain fell year round. The dense forest blocked
out the sun. Underneath the trees, it always seemed to be dusk,
because little light could shine through.

Snakes, insects, and wild animals discouraged all but the bravest
adventurers from entering the forests. Even the smallest creatures

could be deadly. For instance, the African tsetse fly carried sleeping sickness. Those who were bit by the tsetse fly went to sleep and never woke up. Soon, they died. Mosquitoes swarmed everywhere, carrying malaria and yellow fever.

Tsetse fly

Kingdoms Grow Out of the Jungle

African societies learned how to live in harmony with nature. They discovered herbal medicines that helped them to fight disease. They developed methods for raising cattle and growing crops. They learned how to mine metals from the earth, and how to make the metals into useful tools and beautiful jewelry. They mastered hunting in the grasslands and in the deep jungles.

They also created complex religions. By worshipping their gods, they showed their wonder and respect for the natural spirits they sensed around them. And they built cities, states, and kingdoms that rivaled any in the world.

About 3,000 years ago, people in Africa learned how to heat up iron and mold it into the shapes they wanted. This is called "forging" metal. By forging, the Africans could create iron tools that made hunting and farming much easier. The population grew as more and more food could be produced. Soon, central and southern Africa were filled with travelers. These travelers were seeking places to start their own societies.

Eventually, the huge continent of Africa was filled with thousands of societies. Many of these societies were very isolated. They took care of their own members and did not communicate with other groups. Because these groups did not talk with one another, each developed its own language. At this time, there were over 1,000 different languages in Africa. Each group also developed its own ideas about nature, about religion, and

Dogon wooden mask

about how people should behave. Artwork varied widely from one region to the next. For instance, tribes in the western part of the Sudan produced an abundance of rich sculptures. In the eastern part of Sudan, on

Mask for a child dancer

the other hand, most groups focused on music and oral literature. These songs and stories were handed down from one generation to the next.

By the tenth century, African cities were bustling with merchants, artists, laborers, and scholars. Great feasts and celebrations were held regularly. Busy cities traded with one another over well-traveled roads. Africans traded a steady supply of gold with European countries.

Over the centuries, slave traders and other prejudiced people have told many false stories about Africa.

Huge statues stand at the entrance to temples cut into sandstone rock on the Nile River.

They thought that African societies were not nearly as advanced as those of Europe. They thought that Africans were not capable of governing themselves, or of making great art. In the past 100 years, however, archaeologists have discovered a different story. Much evidence shows that African societies were flourishing several hundred years ago. This evidence includes cave paintings, tales and songs passed down by word of mouth, and the masks, dolls, and clothing used in religious ceremonies. Many experts believe that Africa was in its golden age when the European slave traders arrived in the 1400s. But this golden age would soon turn to dust.

Wall carving at a temple along the Nile River.

17

Early map of Africa

CHAPTER 2

THE MERCHANT KINGDOMS OF AFRICA

Ghana

It is said that Kanissa'ia, the King of Ghana, owned 1,000 horses. Each horse slept on a mattress and was tended by three servants. Every evening, the great king would come out of his palace and speak to his subjects. One thousand logs roared on a giant bonfire. The king sat upon a throne of gleaming gold and spoke while food was prepared for 1,000 people.

The ancient kingdom of Ghana was built on the Niger River in what are now Mali and Mauritania. (In Africa today, there is a country that is also called Ghana. It is about 800 miles south of the ancient kingdom.) Ghana was the first of several empires that were built on the grasslands of north-central Africa. This area is known as the Sudan. The kingdoms of Ghana were probably founded in the 300s. Ghana became increasingly powerful, starting around 700. In the 1200s, the Mali Empire replaced it as the most powerful kingdom.

What we know of the history of Ghana is based on the writings of Arab travelers. Iron, gold, and salt were the products that fueled the rise of the kingdom of Ghana. The people of Ghana used iron to make swords, daggers, iron weapons, and arrows. In the year 1067, an Arab scholar wrote that, "the king of Ghana could put 200,000 warriors in the field, more than 40,000 of them armed with bows and arrows." Another scholar wrote that Ghana's neighbors "know not iron, and fight with bars of ebony wood. The Ghanians defeat them because they fight with swords and lances." With so much fierce fighting power, Ghana quickly overran the neighboring societies. Ghana then took control of these groups' resources, including their gold.

Along the Senegal River, there lived a tribe of people who loved salt. These people were of the Ferawi (pronounced Fur-ah'-we) tribe. Although they loved to add salt to their dishes, the Ferawi had none. What they did have, however, were mines filled with gold.

Gold

Camels are used to haul cars of salt along a track at an extraction site.

They would trade one ounce of gold for one ounce of salt, because they loved the taste so much.

North of Ghana lay vast salt mines. Arab traders from the Middle East would travel thousands of miles on camelback, bringing salt from these mines to Ghana. They wanted to trade this salt for gold. The Ferawi, who lived southwest of Ghana, would bring their gold north to Ghana. They wanted to trade their gold for salt. In this way, Ghana became a central place where people who wanted gold and people who wanted salt could meet and make trades. The residents of Ghana controlled the roads that these traders used. In order to use the roads, the traders had to pay taxes to Ghana, in the form of gold, copper, cloth, and dried fruit.

The Ghanians built large, comfortable cities of stone. Their markets were filled with dates, olives, fruit, and grain. In the south, "salt cities" prospered. In these cities, people built their homes out of thick slabs of salt. The roofs were made of camel skin.

Throughout the centuries, several groups of armed invaders attacked Ghana. There were many years of hardship and decay, while the people of Ghana tried to ward off these intruders. The Arab Muslims tried to force the Ghanians to convert to their religion many times. In 1203, the Sosso tribe attacked Ghana and turned its people into slaves. Ghana became a weak and powerless country. Its capital city was destroyed in 1235.

Mali

Sundiata (Sun-di-ah'-ta) Keita was the leader of the Sosso tribe when they conquered Ghana. Around the year 1240, Sundiata created a professional army that conquered many lands. His kingdom was called Mali. Ghana became part of the huge new empire of Mali, which was larger than Europe. Like Ghana, Mali's power came from its great supplies of gold, iron, and salt.

In 1312, Sundiata's grandson became the Sultan of Mali. His name was Mansa Musa (Man-sah' Moo'-sah). During Mansa Musa's reign, Mali became famous throughout the Middle East and Europe. Mansa Musa believed in the Islamic religion. In 1324, he decided to make a journey to Mecca, Saudi Arabia, because Mecca was the spiritual homeland of Islam.

Mansa Musa began his pilgrimage to Mecca with a caravan of 60,000 men. Musicians played for him while 500 slaves marched in front of the caravan. Each slave carried a four-pound staff made of pure gold. Trains of camels carried gold and gifts. Everywhere he went, Mansa Musa handed out gold to people in the street. In fact, he gave away so much gold that its value began to drop. But because Mansa Musa was so generous, and because the sight of his caravan was so amazing, he became the subject of wonder and

A mosque in Mopti, Mali, northwestern Africa.

gossip for many years. From Europe to Egypt, Mali was known as a rich and splendid kingdom.

In Mali, Mansa Musa sat on a throne made of ebony. Elephant tusks formed an arch over his throne. Above the tusks, a huge, brightly colored umbrella kept the sun from beating down on the sultan's head. The fearsome executioner stood always by his side. Clustered around Mansa Musa's throne were trumpeters and drummers. Horses stood nearby, adorned with gold and jewels. Soldiers and slaves stood at attention. From this seat of power, Mansa Musa ruled Mali for many years.

Mansa Musa built Mali into a tremendous kingdom. Mali was known all around the world for its wealthy, well-organized cities. The most famous cities were Gao and Timbuktu. Mali was famous for its culture and schools. Mansa Musa also put Mali on the map. Around 1350, European mapmakers started showing Mali on their maps. They also instructed travelers who wanted to journey to the great kingdom.

After Mansa Musa's death, the kingdom of Mali grew weaker. Still, there were many caravan routes for traveling into the city. In one year, 12,000 camels traveled over just one of these caravan routes. Other caravans entered the kingdom from every direction. Mali was a peaceful kingdom. Several visitors wrote that its people believed in justice. They also said that the kingdom was safe. Many travelers said that they felt safer in Mali than in any of the cities in Europe or the Middle East.

The Fabled City of Timbuktu

In the heart of Mali, on the banks of the Niger River, lay the splendid city of Timbuktu (Tim-buk'-too). During Mansa Musa's reign, he ordered Islamic houses of worship, called mosques (mosks), to be built in Timbuktu. The mosques were huge, gorgeous buildings. They had solid-gold domes, velvet rugs, fountains, and artwork carved into stone. The mosques were designed by a Spanish poet. They were said to be as beautiful as any mosques in the world.

Timbuktu was also known as a center for learning. While the Hundred Years War was raging in Europe, Timbuktu was in a golden age of knowledge and wisdom. One traveler wrote, "The king pays great respect for men of learning. More profit is made from the book trade than any other line of business." Law and the Islamic religion were the favorite topics of the wise scholars of Timbuktu.

Timbuktu's glory lasted for several hundred years. Today, no one knows what knowledge the scholars of Timbuktu possessed. Their books have all decayed into dust. But during her glory, Timbuktu was a jeweled city in the golden crown of Mali.

Minarets at the Grande Mosquee in Timbuktu date back to the 14th century.

CHAPTER 3

THE FOREST KINGDOMS OF AFRICA

Artwork of the Jungle

The merchant kingdoms, Ghana and Mali, were built on the dry grasslands of the north. Farther south, these grasslands turned to lush tropical forests. The long rains produced all sorts of thick, beautiful trees and blooming plants. Thousands of species of animals, insects, and birds howled, chirped, and buzzed throughout the forests.

The rainy weather produced an amazing array of beauty, and so did the people who lived in this area. The people who inhabited the forests produced wonderful bronze masks, wood carvings, gold jewelry, and more.

What we know about the merchant kingdoms comes mostly from Arab traders. These traders wrote reports of their trips to Mali and other cities. But few reports were written about life in the forest kingdoms. The thick jungle prevented outsiders from entering and exploring these parts. Therefore, most of what we know about these societies comes from spoken stories that were passed down from one generation to the next. Archaeologists are also digging up information to help us learn about the forest kingdoms.

Palm trees enclose a cove on the coast of Grand Comoro Island in the Mozambique Channel.

The Nok Culture

The oldest culture discovered so far in West Africa is the Nok Culture. Archaeologists in this region have unearthed lifelike statues of humans and animals. These statues are made from terra-cotta, a kind of baked clay. Some of these statues are at least 2,500 years old. The figures are extremely well made. Their heads are three times larger than their bodies. This is probably because the Nok people believed that the brain, eyes, ears, and mouth were the most important parts of a person.

The Nok people seem to have invented African art styles that are still being used in Nigeria. They lived in clay huts in the lowlands and hills. They wore beaded jewelry. These Nok artists disappeared long ago. Only their clay work is left to tell us anything about them.

Yoruba

The Yoruba states, in present-day western Nigeria, were the largest forest kingdoms in West Africa. The Yoruba are the

Bronze figure

descendants of the Nok people. Yoruba artwork includes beautiful bronze and brass masks and statues. In 1897, British archaeologists discovered bronze statues made by the Yoruba long ago. Today, these works of art are ranked among the greatest in the world. Some of the finest ones were probably created in the 1400s. They portray the heads of the great Yoruba kings.

People in Yoruba lived in walled cities. They grew their food in fields that lay outside of the walls. They traded their products with the kingdoms in the north. Cloth and koala nuts were their main products. After the 1500s, the Yoruba people began trading with the Europeans on Africa's west coast. The Europeans came to buy ivory, pepper, and slaves.

The main city in Yoruba was called Benin. The Europeans were impressed with Benin's wide streets and neat rows of houses. A Dutch

Tribal King

visitor in 1602 was also fascinated by the king's palace. He reported that the palace had huge rooms with galleries and courtyards. Giant brass statues decorated every room. The king owned stables with a large number of horses. He also owned slaves. The Dutch visitor watched them carry water, yams, and palm wine for their master.

As the years passed, many people were taken from Benin by the Europeans. They were sent to America and forced to become slaves. By the 1700s, Benin was deserted. Its buildings crumbled into ruin. The countryside was empty and the farmland was overgrown and unused.

TIMELINE

10,000 B.C. Early humans have stone tools, trap animals for food, make pottery, and create cave paintings

4,000–1,500 B.C. Climate changes turning lush forest and grasslands into the present-day Sahara Desert

1,000 B.C. The process of forging metal is discovered

700 The rise of the kingdom of Ghana

900 Trade is widespread among the kingdoms of Africa and the countries of the Mediterranean

1203 Sosso tribe attacks Ghana and enslaves its people

1225–1240 Capital of Ghana is destroyed and Ghana becomes part of the Empire of Mali

1312 Mansa Musa becomes Sultan of Mali

1350s Mali becomes famous throughout the Middle East and Europe for its culture and schools

1400's Slave traders from Europe arrive; slave trade begins

Late 1400s Portuguese explorers discover the kingdom of Zanj on Africa's southeast coast

1500s The Yoruba tribe begins trading with Europeans on Africa's West coast

Early 1700s Capital of Yoruba is deserted after its people are consumed by the slave trade

CHAPTER 4

THE ZANJ KINGDOM OF EAST AFRICA

The Lands of the Zanj

Portuguese explorers sailed down the coast of West Africa in the late 1400s. After they rounded the bottom of the continent at the Cape of Good Hope, they sailed up the eastern coast. Much to their surprise, the Portuguese found beautiful civilizations and towns. They found cities with tall buildings made of stone and coral, white and sparkling in the sun. The Portuguese found ports filled with ships from India and China. Many of the ships were larger and better built than the European ships. The busy trade gave the towns an air of wealth and luxury. The Portuguese were surprised that they were not treated as important guests. The people of the coast were used to visitors arriving from the sea.

Vasco da Gama, the leader of the expedition, wrote this in his diary: "When we had been there for three days, two gentlemen of the country came to see us. They were very haughty and valued nothing we gave them." But the Portuguese "cried with joy" at what they saw and heard in the country. They saw it as a place to make their fortunes.

The area described by the Portuguese was a country called the Land of Zanj. Zanj stretched from present-day Mozambique (Mo-zam-beek') to Kenya and included the island of Madagascar (Mad-ah-gas'-ker).

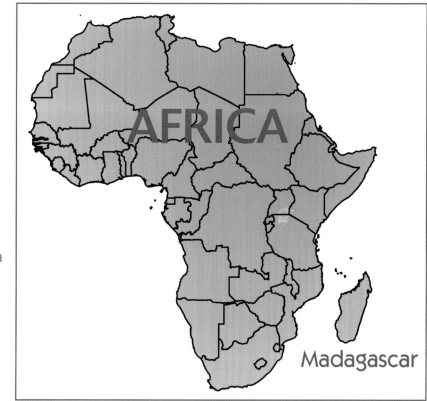

Map of Africa showing the location of Madagascar.

People in Zanj had been trading with China, Arabia, and India for almost 2,000 years. The Zanj people killed elephants for their ivory tusks. They traded the ivory for wheat, rice, sesame oil, cotton cloth, and honey. The Europeans also traded with Zanj. Gold Roman coins from the third century have been found in the sands of Zanj. The Zanj also exported gold, tortoise shells, and slaves. Iron that was mined in Zanj was highly valued in India. Ivory from Zanj was used in China. The Chinese used it to make splendid chairs in which kings were carried.

As the centuries passed, the people of Zanj imported large amounts of cloth and beads from India. Ships arrived from China full of silk, pottery, and porcelain. The pottery from China was very valuable. A shipload of it was worth a great sum of money. Between 1200 and 1500, the wealth that was exchanged between China and Zanj was unequaled anywhere in the world.

The Fall of Zanj

The Portuguese arrival in Zanj was disastrous to the wealthy and peaceful civilizations there. The Portuguese had superior naval and military power. Their men were heavily armed with guns and cannons. They wanted control over the riches of Zanj. They raided

An ivory market at Grahamstown in Cape Colony, South Africa, 1866.

the coastal towns with great cruelty and savageness. The easygoing Zanj people could not resist. The beautiful towns, with centuries of history and culture behind them, were destroyed. Some of the major towns were named Kilwa, Wambasa, Lamu, and Pate. Their citizens were massacred. The gorgeous homes of Zanj were looted and burned by the Portuguese invaders. Today, fragments of pottery and overgrown ruins in the jungle are all that remains of Zanj. Eight years after they arrived, the Portuguese traders totally controlled the coast of Africa.

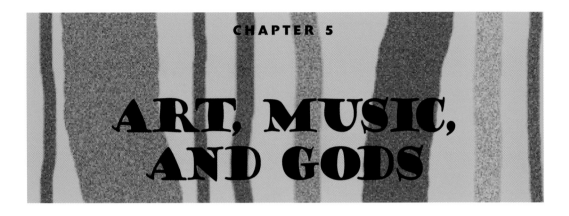

CHAPTER 5

ART, MUSIC, AND GODS

Artists

Most early African art was part of religious worship. African artists used sculpture, music, and dancing to show love and respect for their gods. Many tribes made masks and costumes that were used in religious ceremonies. The Benin people made royal masks, and other tribes made masks that showed the faces of monsters. African artists used many different materials. Some worked with metals like bronze, iron, and gold.

Masks

Others used clay, wood, cloth and iron. Besides sculpture, pots, and masks, they also made jewelry and clothes. These artists showed a great respect for tradition and quality.

Most African sculpture was not meant only to be admired. Each piece was designed to attract religious spirits. Carved dolls were used to hold the spirits of Carved unborn babies. Carved lion drummers were pounded into mask the ground during dances to awaken the spirits in the earth. Geometric patterns were woven into cloth and painted onto faces. Each pattern had its own religious meaning. Masks that were carved to look like animals or mythical beasts were worn during weddings, funerals, and other ceremonies. Sometimes dancers would go into a trance and take on the spirit of the masks they wore. Masked dancers, feeling themselves possessed by strange spirits, would dance for hours.

Many artists also made cups, stools, spoons, and knives for every day use.

A wood cut figure representing a woman with her newborn baby.

The Power of the Gods

There are almost as many African gods as there are African tribes. Nearly all Africans believed in a single "High God" from whom all things flowed. Beneath the High God, lesser gods ruled human affairs. Africans had gods for almost everything that affected their lives. They worshiped the gods of storms, mountains, rivers, the sun, trees, lions, and many others.

Within every tribe, several people were believed to be able to communicate with the gods. Often, these people were skilled in the art of physical and mental healing. Some used plants and herbs as cures for illnesses.

Africans also worshiped their ancestors. Many dances, songs, and works of art were used to contact relatives who had died. Many African tribes believed in sorcery and witchcraft. There was good magic and bad magic. They often used witch doctors to help them break evil spells or avoid bad luck.

African witch doctor

Over the centuries, both invaders and friendly visitors have brought their own religions into Africa. Christianity and Islam, for instance, have been a part of African life for many hundreds of years. In many places, these faiths have mingled with native beliefs to produce a deep understanding of spiritual life.

The Dance and Drums of Africa

To many Africans, dancing was the most important part of their ceremonies. Dancing was a way to combine religion and everyday

matters. There were dances to mark the beginning of a hunt, and there were dances to mark the end of a hunt. Harvests, marriages, holidays, gods, goddesses, and religious ceremonies all had their own dances. At the heart of all African dances was the drum.

Two Malians wear elaborate masks as they perform a ritual dance.

Long ago, African drummers pounded on rocks. Later on, they discovered how to stretch hides over hollow logs to make drums. A good African drummer could make his drum "speak" in words and sentences that the other tribe members could understand. Drums were used to send messages from one village to the next. A drummer from one village would drum out a loud message. The drummer in the next village would listen and

Group of dancers and stilt walkers perform in Mali, West Africa.

pass it on to the next tribe. In this way, a drum message could be sent 100 miles in only two hours. Many drums were considered sacred. These special drums were used only in certain religious ceremonies.

A Final Word

African culture thrived between the tenth and sixteenth centuries. But when the Europeans came to Africa, beginning in the late 1400s, they destroyed almost everything they found. Once the slave trade started, much of Africa's population was sold into slavery. Scholars estimate that as many as 10 million people were kidnapped from their homelands. Many of these kidnapped Africans died on ships, on their way to becoming slaves.

Many of the Europeans who traveled to Africa were slave traders. They earned huge sums of money by selling the African people into slavery. These traders did not want others to know about the wonderful cultures of Africa. In the 1500s, therefore, most Europeans did not know how many scholars, artists, and advanced societies Africa contained. They thought Africa was a wild jungle filled with savages. Even today, such wrong ideas have not been completely erased.

One book cannot describe all the different and wonderful faces of Africa. Your local library has many more books about the people, customs, and art of Africa. By learning more about these, we can make the history of Africa come alive.

V asco da Gama was a Portuguese explorer who traveled to Africa in 1497. The map below shows his route.

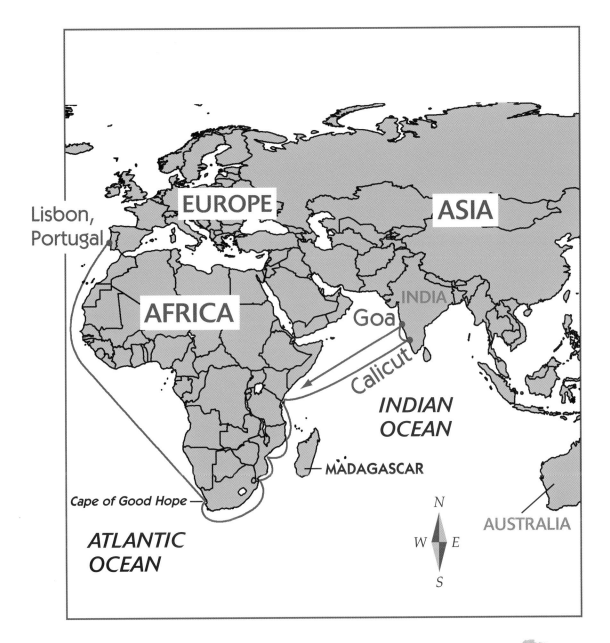

INTERNET SITES

Odyssey

http://www.emory.edu/CARLOS/ODYSSEY

Learn about all aspects of ancient African life through maps, artwork, and interactive games. Check out the rituals and ceremonies, daily life, and communication of different tribes.

Civilizations in Africa—The Hausa Kingdoms

www.wsu.edu:8080/~dee/CIVAFRCA/HAUSA.HTM

See histories and timelines of the tribes of Ancient Africa.

Collapse—Why Do Civilizations Fall?

www.learner.org/exhibits/collapse/

Read about some of the greatest civilizations in world history and how they disappeared. Check out the interactive exercises and links to related pages.

GLOSSARY

Anthropologist—Scientists who study the history of mankind and its various societies and cultures.

Archaeologist—Scientists that dig in ancient civilizations searching for artifacts and clues to a culture's existence.

B.C.—This abbreviation is short for "Before Christ." It is used to describe the time period before the birth of Jesus Christ.

Caravan—A company of travelers or merchants on a long journey through desert or hostile territory.

Climate—The average weather pattern of an area over time.

Customs—The uses, practices, and conventions that regulate social life in a given society. The manner and method of everyday life.

Dawn Ape—Fruit-eating creature that roamed the forests of North Africa 33 million years ago. Although it looked more like a cat, its bone structure was similar to that of human beings. Scientists discovered its remains in 1985 and believe it is the oldest direct ancestor of humans.

Droughts—A period of dryness causing extensive damage to crops or preventing their growth. Droughts could be devastating to ancient cultures who depended on farming survival.

Ebony—A hard, heavy, durable wood found in the tropical areas of Asia and Africa.

Forging—A method of shaping metal by heating it up enough to bend and mold. Africans used this technique to create tools that made farming and hunting easier. The increase in food supplies allowed the African population to grow steadily.

Herbal Medicines—Treatments for disease found in the plant life of the local area. They were most abundant in forest areas.

Islam—One of the five major religions of the world. Followers of Islam, called Muslims, are required to make a pilgrimage to Mecca, Saudi Arabia, the spiritual homeland of Islam and its god Allah.

Ivory—The cream-white, bone-like material that makes up the tusks of elephants. Ivory was a very valuable product in the ancient civilizations of Africa, and was traded with Eastern countries for wheat, rice, cloth, pottery, and oils.

Kingdom—A politically organized community headed by a king or queen.

Malaria—Disease transmitted by mosquitoes that causes chills and fever as a result of the destruction of red blood cells. The disease is still commonplace in underdeveloped nations.

Merchant—A person who buys and sells commodities and products for a profit.

Mines—A pit in the earth from which minerals, such as coal, salt, and gold, are taken for use in society.

Mosque—An Islamic place of worship. Many mosques were elaborately decorated with large, gold domes, enormous fountains, and beautiful artwork.

Pilgrimage—A journey to a shrine or sacred place. Followers of the Islamic religion are supposed to make a pilgrimage to Mecca, the birthplace of the prophet Muhammad, at least once in their lives.

Relief—A mode of sculpture in which forms and figures are distinguished from a surrounding surface by molding, chipping, or cutting away of the surface.

Slave Trade—The buying and selling of blacks for profit prior to the American Civil War. The slave trade was responsible for taking about 10 million blacks from Africa to work on farms and plantations in the United States and Caribbean.

Sub-Saharan Africa—The area on the African continent south of the Sahara Desert. This area is twice the size of the United States.

Sudan—The grasslands of North-Central Africa.

Terra-Cotta—A kind of baked clay used for artwork and dwellings in the Nok culture of West Africa.

Yellow Fever—Disease transmitted by mosquitoes in tropical and sub-tropical areas that causes hemorrhaging in the stomach, fever, and eventually death.

INDEX